FROGS & TOADS

Helen Riley

PUFFIN BOOKS

CONTENTS

1. Different sizes

Compared to other **vertebrates**, frogs and toads are all on the small side. Like all **amphibians**, frogs and toads are cold-blooded animals. That means that the temperature of their bodies does not remain constant, but changes as the temperature of their surroundings changes. Frogs and toads rely on heat from their surroundings to warm their bodies up, so it is better to be small because a small body takes less time to warm up.

The biggest **species** of frog is the goliath frog, which lives in the rain forests of West Africa. This shy creature can measure up to 75 cm with its back legs out-stretched. Goliath frogs live in deep pools in rivers in the African forests. As the goliath frog is so big, local people often hunt it for food. They believe that the goliath frog's leg bones have magical powers to bring good luck.

One of the smallest species of frog or toad is the pygmy golden frog from Brazil. It measures less than 2.5 cm in length. This tiny frog lives among the dead leaves on the floor of the forest.

Below The goliath frog is the world's largest frog.

Right A pygmy golden frog from the rain forests of Brazil.

2. Strange shapes

Some species of frogs and toads have very strange shapes. Although they may look very odd their bodies have adapted (changed) for a special reason.

The spatulate nosed tree frog from Central America has a long nose with a wide flattened end, a bit like a spoon. It uses its nose to lift up sections of the bark of trees. The frog then crawls into the hole it has made and uses the end of its nose to block up the entrance. Sealed safely inside its hole, the spatulate nosed tree frog is safe from **predators**.

Most frogs and toads live on land as well as in water and so they breathe air through their **lungs**. The Lake Titicaca frog spends all of its life underwater, so its body has adapted in a very unusual way. Unlike most other frogs and toads it has no lungs. Instead, it breathes through its skin. The Lake Titicaca frog has large folds of skin that drape from the sides of its body. These extra folds increase the surface area of its skin, so that there is a larger area over which it can absorb (take in) as much **oxygen** from the water as it needs.

Left A spatulate nosed tree frog showing off its long, upturned snout.

Below The Lake Titicaca frog's loose skin drapes from its sides.

3.   Long jumpers and high-fliers

The ability to suddenly jump a long distance is a good way of escaping predators. Frogs and toads have strong, long hind (back) legs that are used for leaping on land. Some species are incredibly **agile**.

The American leopard frog, for example, can jump up to thirteen times its own length. Just imagine a human long jumper being able to do the same.

Tree frogs are also good leapers. They often have to jump to catch insects in flight. They have suction pads on the under-sides of their feet that enable them to cling to wherever they land.

Gliding tree frogs, which live in the rain forests of South America and Asia, jump the longest distances. When trying to avoid a predator they launch themselves from a tree into the air. To help them travel in the air they spread the webs of skin between the toes of their enormous hind feet. In this way they can glide long distances from tree to tree, or to the ground.

Below This gliding frog has webs of skin between the toes of its feet.

Right The back legs of the leopard frog are very long.

4. A bite to eat

Predators, such as rats and snakes, often hunt frogs and toads, but the larger species of frogs and toads may turn the tables on their enemies.

The South American horned frog, with its large mouth and sharp teeth, is a fierce predator. It regularly hunts and eats small **mammals** and snakes. In Argentina, it was believed that if a horned frog bit the lip of a grazing horse, the horse would die from the bite. This cannot be true because the horned frog does not have **poison** in its mouth, but it shows the boldness of this creature that is willing to attack animals many times its own size.

Frogs and toads will sometimes eat other frogs and toads of the same or a different species. This may seem quite shocking, but it is not surprising if you consider that frogs and toads are not fussy about what they eat. They will eat any animal that moves and is small enough to fit into their mouths.

Left The horned frog crushes its prey to death with its strong jaws.

Below A smoky jungle frog eating a puddle frog whole.

5. Disappearing acts

A good way to avoid a predator is to make sure you are difficult to see. Some species of frogs and toads rely on **camouflage** to protect them from enemies.

The European green tree frog blends into the leaves of the plants on which it lives. If it moves to a new position on a plant, it can change its colour very rapidly from bright green to brown to match its new surroundings. It does this by altering the distribution of coloured **pigments** in its skin.

The Asian leaf frog has a more permanent disguise. It lives on the forest floor and looks just like a dead leaf. Its flattened body is a golden brown colour, with pointed 'horns' over its eyes and a pointed nose. It even has ridges on its back that look like the veins of a leaf.

Below The horns of the Asian leaf frog hide its eyes from predators.

Right The camouflage of this European tree frog perfectly matches the leaf.

6. Warning colours

Poison arrow frogs are beautiful but deadly. Their bright colours are a warning to predators because they have **glands** in their skin that contain very strong poison. The poison has a **paralyzing** effect on mammals, and is strong enough to kill a small creature, such as a mouse. Poison arrow frogs live in the rain forests of South America. Local people collect the poison from the frogs' skins and smear it on the tips of their hunting arrows. They use the poison-tipped arrows to catch animals for food.

Fire-bellied toads combine camouflage with warning colours to protect themselves. The upper surfaces of their bodies are dark coloured and blend in well with the muddy pools where they live. In contrast, the lower surfaces of the toads' bodies are bright orange. When fire-bellied toads are threatened they throw themselves on to their backs and show their brightly coloured bellies. The shock of the sudden flash of colour is usually enough to scare off a predator.

Left Predators know that poison arrow frogs are poisonous and avoid them.

Below You can see why the fire-bellied toad got its name.

7. Serenading

Male frogs and toads are very noisy during the **mating season**. They gather at **breeding ponds** and 'sing' to attract females. They make sounds using **vocal sacs** in the bottom of their mouths. By breathing air into their lungs, closing their mouths and nostrils, and pumping air into and out of the sacs they can make loud noises.

The great plains toad of North America has one of the longest lasting calls known. It lasts for several minutes non-stop. This toad has a single, large, sausage-shaped vocal sac. Frogs and toads can call continually for long periods without running out of breath because they breathe through their skins as well as with their lungs.

The varying calls of the barking tree frog tell the female where the male is and if he is ready to **mate**. The 'true' barking call is heard only when the male is in the trees. Once he has entered the water his call changes. So the female knows when the male has entered the pond.

Below When filled with air, the vocal sac of the great plains toad is almost as big as its body.

Right The barking tree frog is so-called because its call sounds like the bark of a dog.

8. Strange places to lay eggs

Most frogs and toads live on land as adults, but return to the water to **spawn**. You may have seen frog and toad spawn in ponds and rivers during early spring.

However, American grey tree frogs lay their eggs in trees which overhang ponds. The female makes a nest of foam from a special liquid she produces from her body. She beats the liquid up into a froth with her hind legs, with a little help from the male. The eggs are laid in the mass of foam, the outside of which soon hardens in the hot sun. The **tadpoles** hatch a few days later. They break out of the crust of the foam nest and fall into the water below.

Glass frogs of Central and South America lay their eggs on leaves which overhang water. Glass frogs are unusual because both the males and the females stay with the eggs, guarding over them and making sure they do not dry out. When the tadpoles have hatched they tumble into the water below.

Left This male glass frog is guarding the eggs.

Below This group of grey tree frogs are all laying eggs in the same foam nest.

9. All change

One of the most amazing things about frogs and toads is the complete change, called **metamorphosis**, they go through from eggs to fully-grown adults. The eggs normally hatch into tadpoles which live in water.

They look completely different from adults. Tadpoles have no legs when they first hatch, they swim using their tails, and they breathe through **gills**. As they metamorphose, they gradually lose their tails and develop legs.

Adult frogs and toads will often eat tadpoles if they come across them. This does not happen often because the adults live on land and the young develop in the water. However, tadpoles of the paradoxical frog need not worry about bumping into adults. The tadpoles are three times as big as the adult paradoxical frogs! Tadpoles of this species may grow to 20 cm long, whereas the adults are only 6 cm long.

For some species the tadpole stage takes place inside the eggs. South American rain frogs lay their eggs on leaves. The eggs contain lots of **yolk** which the tadpoles feed on as they develop. They do not emerge from the eggs until they have changed into fully-formed tiny froglets.

Below The paradoxical tadpole shrinks when it becomes an adult.

Right A tiny rain froglet still encased in its egg.

10.   Good fathers

In some species of frog and toad it is the male that takes on the job of caring for the eggs or young.

Male midwife toads carry their eggs around with them until they hatch.

After the male and female have mated, the male winds the string of eggs around his back legs. For the next month or so he carries the eggs around with him. He spends the daylight hours secreted away in a dark, damp place, and emerges at night to feed and dampen the eggs in dew or in a pond. When the tadpoles are ready to hatch, the male takes them down to a suitable pond and allows them to swim away.

In the case of the Darwin's frog from South America the female lays the eggs on the ground and the male stays with the eggs until the tadpoles hatch. Then the male Darwin's frog swallows the young – not into his stomach, but into his vocal sacs. The tadpoles develop for two to three months inside their father, and emerge through his mouth as tiny, fully-formed froglets.

Left This tiny Darwin's frog has come out from the vocal sac of its father.

Below A male midwife toad carrying a string of eggs.

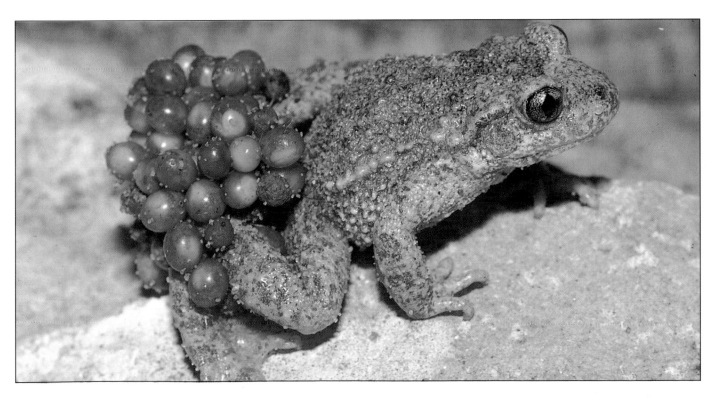

11. Froggy-back rides

Strawberry poison arrow frogs lay their eggs in small pools of water at the bases of bromeliad leaves. Both the male and female parents stay close to the tadpoles as they develop. If the water in the leaves looks as though it will dry up, they carry the tadpoles away on their backs to a new pool.

Marsupial frogs also carry their tadpoles around on their backs, but underneath their skins. When the marsupial frogs mate, the male (which is much smaller than the female) sits on top of the female's back. The female leans forward so that her back slopes upward from her head. She lays eggs one at a time, and the male **fertilizes** them with his **sperm**. The eggs then roll forwards into a pouch on the female's back. About twenty eggs are laid in all. When they have developed into small froglets, the young emerge from the pouch to start life on their own.

Below These marsupial froglets have just been 'born' from the pouch on their mother's back.

Right A female strawberry poison arrow frog carrying tadpoles around on her back.

24

12. Underground havens

Frogs and toads use their skins to help them breathe. Air can only pass through the skin when it is moist, so most species live in damp places. Some species, though, manage to survive in dry places.

Spadefoot toads live in hot, dry areas in North America and Europe. They stop themselves from drying out by burrowing underground. To help them dig, they have horny pads on their hind feet.

Spadefoot toads can stay in their burrows for weeks or months at a time without feeding. The only time they emerge from their burrows is at night after a rainfall.

Australian water-holding frogs also live in dry places and burrow to keep themselves from drying out. They take up so much water into their **bladders** and into spaces underneath their skins that they swell right up. To prevent water being lost through their skins, they cover themselves with a clear, waterproof 'coat'. During the dry season, **Aborigines** dig for water-holding frogs so they can drink their water.

Left A spadefoot toad emerges from its burrow after rain.

Below This water-holding frog is removing its waterproof skin.

13. A watery world

Rather than living on land, frogs and toads of some species live entirely in water.

South American Surinam toads have flattened bodies and long sensitive fingers on their front feet. They use their fingers to feel for food in the muddy waters. Any small animal they find is seized, and crammed straight into their mouths.

Adult African clawed toads also spend virtually their entire lives in water. Unlike most frogs and toads, the adults have special **organs**, called lateral lines. This organ, which is also found in fish, allows them to detect movements in the water. These movements might be from a small creature like an **aquatic** insect, which the frog could eat. Or, they could be from a large fish which might try to eat the frog. The lateral line therefore helps the clawed toad to find food or escape predators.

Below Surinam toads use their fingers to find food under water.

Right African clawed toads hunt for food below the surface of the water.

GLOSSARY

Aborigines The original people of Australia.

Agile Being able to move quickly.

Amphibians A group of animals that includes frogs, toads, newts and salamanders. Most amphibians start life as tadpoles that live in water and change into adults that live mainly on land.

Aquatic Animals that live in water.

Bladder The place in an animal's body where waste liquid, urine, is stored before being passed out of the body.

Breeding pond The place where, after the male and female frog or toad have mated, the fertilized eggs are left.

Camouflage The colours and patterns on the body which help the animal to blend with its surroundings.

Fertilize When a male's sperm joins with a female's egg. The fertilized egg then develops into a new individual.

Gills The feather-like structures used by fish and tadpoles to breathe under water.

Gland An organ in an animal's body that produces special substances, such as poison.

Lungs The organs inside an animal's body that are used for breathing air.

Mammals A group of warm-blooded animals. The females feed their young with milk produced from their own bodies.

Mate The act performed by a male and female of a species in order to produce young.

Mating season The time of year certain species of animal mate.

Metamorphosis The series of changes that take place during the development of a frog's or toad's egg into an adult.

Organ A part of an animal's body that performs a particular important job e.g. the lungs breathe in air which contains oxygen.

Oxygen A type of gas that all animals need to breathe in order to live.

Paralyzing To make an animal unable to move and therefore helpless.

Pigment The colouring substance in the skin of an animal or surface of a plant.

Poison Any substance which, when swallowed or taken into the body, causes harm or kills.

Predators Animals that hunt other animals for food.

Spawn To lay eggs. The eggs of frogs and toads are also called spawn.

Species A particular kind of plant or animal.

Sperm The male sex cells which fertilize the eggs of a female.

Tadpole The young of frogs or toads. They usually hatch from eggs and live in water. Their bodies are very different to how they will look as adults.

Vertebrate An animal with a backbone.

Vocal sac A pocket of skin at the bottom of the mouth of a frog or toad. Often used to make mating calls.

Yolk The part of an egg that provides food for the young to hatch and begin to grow.

Picture Acknowledgements

All pictures in this book were provided by Oxford Scientific Films Ltd: G I Bernard 13, S C Bisserot 20, S Dalton 9, M Fogden cover, 5, 11, 12, 16, 18, 19, 21, 22, 24, 25, J Frazier 27, Z Leszczynski 4, 6, 7, 8, 10, 14, 15, 17, 26, 29, M Linley 23, A Ramage 28.

INDEX

Numbers in **bold** indicate photographs.